ONE NIGHT IN NOVEMBER

ONE NIGHT IN NOVEMBER

by Alan Pollock

JOSEF WEINBERGER PLAYS

LONDON

ONE NIGHT IN NOVEMBER
First published in 2008
by Josef Weinberger Ltd
12-14 Mortimer Street
London W1T 3JJ
www.josef-weinberger.com
general.info@jwmail.co.uk

ISBN   978 0 85676 301 4 (13 digit)

Printed by Commercial Colour Press plc, Hainault, Essex

For Liz

One Night In November was first presented at the Belgrade Theatre, Coventry (Hamish Glen, Artistic Director, Joanna Reid, Executive Director) on 11th March 2008. The cast was as follows:

MICHAEL GREEN	Daniel Brocklebank
KATIE STANLEY	Joanna Christie
JACK STANLEY	Tony Turner
MARGARET STANLEY	Helen Sheals
JOAN STANLEY	Ellie Paskell
KEN WIDDOWS	Aran Bell
SHEILA ARBUTHNOT	Leandra Ashton
RONALD CAVE	David Acton
HILDE CHAMBERS	Leandra Ashton
JOHN MARTIN	Richard Franklin
HERBET MORRISON	David Acton

Directed by Hamish Glen
Designed by Patrick Connellan
Lighting Design by Arnim Freiss
Sound Design by John Scott

CHARACTERS

MICHAEL GEEEN – Linguist at Bletchley Park

KATIE STANLEY – Clerk

JACK STANLEY – Shop steward and factory worker

MARGARET STANLEY – Waitress

JOAN STANLEY – Wages secretary

KEN WIDDOWS – ARP Warden

SHEILA ARBUTHNOT – Linguist at Bletchley Park

RONALD CAVE – Section Head, Bletchley Park

HILDE CHAMBERS – Journalist (played by the actor playing SHEILA)

JOHN MARTIN – Private Secretary to Winston Churchill

A POLECEMAN (actor playing CAVE)

HERBERT MORRISON (actor plaing CAVE)

PETER (actor playing MARTIN)

Others roles played by the company

The play takes place in various locations around Coventry, and at Bletchley Park, in October and November 1940, and very briefly, in both 1941 and 1976.

The settings are intended to be fluid and indicative, and the play is to be performed by a company of nine actors with the doubling as indicated above.

ACT ONE

A woman of indeterminate age – KATIE STANLEY *– wearing
trousers, her hair tied back, faces an elderly man with a
watering can –* JOHN MARTIN. *The year is 1976.*

MARTIN   As Palmerston once said of another matter.
                Only three men ever understood the problem.
                Of these, one died. One went mad, and the
                other one was me. I've forgotten.

KATIE   You were his Principal Private Secretary.

MARTIN   Mutatis mutandis . . . what do you hope to gain
                by this?

KATIE   You were the *only* other person present . . .

MARTIN   I'm really not sure what I can do for you. Mrs –

KATIE   Miss.

MARTIN   Miss Stanley.

                (*Pause.*)

KATIE   (*turning to the audience*) I suppose what it
                amounts to . . . what it's always been about, for
                me, is why? At the time, at any rate, it all
                seemed perfectly straightforward. I met Michael
                on the platform at Henley in Arden station . . .

                (*A young man stands on a railway platform.
                the woman –* KATIE STANLEY *– steps forward,
                releasing her hair as she does so. It is now
                autumn 1940.*)

MICHAEL   Where am I?

KATIE   I suppose it's alright to say . . . this is Henley
                in Arden.

MICHAEL   I like your trousers.

KATIE   My trousers? (*To audience.*) I'd been to visit
           my aunt. To help her in the garden. Digging for
           Victory, we called it.

MICHAEL   (*a twinkle*) Like Rosalind. 'A gallant curtle axe
           upon my thigh, a boar spear in my hand . . .'

KATIE   (*puzzled*) What?

MICHAEL   Our train broke down. We were brought here
           on a bus. Then another came, full of soldiers.
           Hardly room to stand up, let alone sit.

KATIE   Where are you trying to get to?

MICHAEL   Birmingham.

KATIE   In that case . . . you're on the wrong platform

MICHAEL   Why did you . . . ?

KATIE   Sorry . . .

MICHAEL   Did you think . . . I might be a spy?

KATIE   (*blushing*) No . . .

MICHAEL   You should ask me a question.

KATIE   A question?

MICHAEL   Ask me to pronounce Leominster.

KATIE   *Leominster*?

MICHAEL   Isn't that what they do?

KATIE   (*to audience*) I'd never met anyone like him . . .

MICHAEL   Would you like a piece of chocolate?

(MICHAEL *pulls an opened packet from his pocket and offers her a piece. They eat in silence for a second.*)

KATIE   What makes you say I'm like Rosalind?

MICHAEL   Rosalind dressed as a boy. When she went to live in Arden.

KATIE   (*tentative*) In . . . *As you like it*?

MICHAEL   *Yes!* Have you read it?

KATIE   I ought to have done. Next year I'm going to Coventry 'Tech. To learn to be an English teacher.

MICHAEL   An English teacher, eh?

KATIE   Are you a soldier?

MICHAEL   No.

KATIE   What are you?

MICHAEL   I'm a Tutor in Romantic Literature.

KATIE   In *Birmingham*?

MICHAEL   No, in Oxford.

(*A moment, as* KATIE *absorbs this. The sound of a train arriving.*)

KATIE   That's my train.

MICHAEL   That's a pity.

KATIE   Why is it? (*To audience.*) He seemed to want to say something.

MICHAEL   (*as the noise of the train gets louder*) Can I just say?

KATIE   (*cupping her ear*) What?

MICHAEL   Can I just say that you're the prettiest girl I've
             ever seen in my life . . .

KATIE   (*the noise is deafening*) What?

             (*The long low moan of an air raid siren
             begins.*)

MICHAEL   Drat.

KATIE   (*to audience*) Had he really just said what I
             thought he had?

MICHAEL   What are we going to do now?

VOICE   (*off*) All change . . .

             (*Pause.*)

KATIE   We could go and find a shelter.

MICHAEL   Then what?

KATIE   And then, when it's a little less noisy . . .
             (*Shyly.*) . . . you can have another go at saying
             what you just said to me now.

             (*A moment between them.*)

KATIE   (*to audience*) Whoever it was that said, 'He
             loved not at all that loved not at first sight'
             had it just about right.

MICHAEL   I don't even know your name.

KATIE   It's Katie.

MICHAEL   I'm Michael.

KATIE   (*to audience*) By the time they sounded the All
             Clear, the last train to Birmingham had gone . . .

Lights up on the interior of an ordinary, end terrace house, in Bramble Street, Coventry. Enter MEG – KATIE'S *mother, a careworn woman in her mid forties – and* JOANIE – KATIE'S *sister, a pretty, slightly younger girl.*

KATIE   I'm still not quite sure how we got there . . .

MEG   Come in, come in.

                 (*Enter a well-built, but limping man,* JACK, *followed by another man in ARP uniform.* KEN.)

JACK   What's that supposed to mean?

KEN   I'm not saying anything –

JACK   Implying . . .

KEN   I just made a little joke, that's all –

KATIE   You're supposed to be resting that foot.

KEN   (*laconic*) He's supposed to be building magnetos for aircraft engines, that's what he's supposed to be doing.

KATIE   (*to audience*) Me, a clerk in the Births Marriages and Deaths Department. Him an Oxford don working for the Government.

MEG   (*to* MICHAEL) Ham sandwiches, will that do you?

MICHAEL   Um . . .

MEG   Katie's brought home a friend.

JACK   (*ignoring her*) Just because there's a war on doesn't mean there always will be, and it doesn't mean people can take liberties.

KEN   I totally agree with you!

JACK   Remember, some of us weren't lucky enough to
             have nice cushy railway jobs back in the early
             nineteen thirties.

JOANIE   I'm Joanie. I'm the sister.

JACK   Dilution's fine if it's for a reason, and if it's for
             the duration. But if we don't set our caps now
             then we're fooling ourselves. Fine if you tell me
             I've got to have two unskilled men working
             next to me.

JOANIE   Or women –

JACK   Fine if you tell me they get paid the same rate.
             But *wartime conditions only*, otherwise what
             happens? When all this blows over you've got
             ten men someone's gone and agreed are all at
             same level and now there's only two jobs for
             them to do.

KEN   Which is how the irresistible force of your Size
             Twelve boot came to be meeting the immovable
             object of your Foreman's office wall?

JACK   Same goes for the shelters. *If the communists
             don't argue the case, who will do?*

KATIE   (*to audience*) I don't think he had any idea
             what he was walking into. Dad was shop
             steward at the British Thompson Huston
             Factory in Ford Street. And a party member.

             (*Pause.*)

JACK   We all fight our wars in different ways.
             (*Beat.*) There's folks sitting in hotels in
             Cheltenham and Harrogate – what's the war to
             them? One less egg with their breakfast and a
             tidy little side-line in war bonds.

KEN   It was a joke, Jack. And not a very good one.
            Now let it lie.

JACK   I do a difficult job and I do it bloody well.

KEN   No one's saying any different.

            (*Beat.*)

MEG   What do you do, Michael?

MICHAEL   Um . . . (*A long silence.*) . . . I'm a translator.

            (*More silence while everyone absorbs this.*)

KATIE   (*pause*) It's not about how we fight the war,
            anyway, it's about *what* we're fighting for –
            isn't it?

JACK   Now she's contradicting us.

KATIE   No one's contradicting anyone.

KEN   You can see how she's going to be a teacher.

JACK   I don't care what anyone says, this is a bosses
            war. Isn't that right, Michael? (*Beat.*) They're
            not running these factories out of the kindness
            of their hearts.

MICHAEL   This is a People's War – isn't it?

            (*Beat.*)

KATIE   Michael's from Birmingham.

JACK   You don't sound like a Brummie.

KATIE   What does a Brummie sound like?

JACK   They're all in it together. You know Churchill's
            got interests in Czechoslovakia? The Skoda
            factory the Nazis have taken over. Pound to a

                         penny not one allied bomb lands on that
                         factory. Not one.

MEG   (*hands* MICHAEL *a round of sandwiches*) Here.

MICHAEL   (*hesitating*) Thank you.

MEG   Well go on then, get stuck in.

                 (*Pause.*)

                 What's the matter?

                 (*Pause. Everyone stares.*)

                 What's the matter?

MICHAEL   I don't eat ham.

MEG   Everyone eats ham.

KEN   Except the A-rabs. And the Jews.

                 (*Beat.*)

KATIE   (*to audience*) I don't think any of us had even
                 met a Jew before.

                 (*Long pause.*)

JACK   So what *do* you do lad?

KATIE   (*to audience*) In the days that followed, we all
                 tried to guess. German agent. Spy. Government
                 inspector. All he'd say was it was about an
                 hour away on the train. And the place he
                 worked in was freezing.

                 (KATIE *pulls* MICHAEL *aside.*)

KATIE   (*whispers*) So what do you think?

MICHAEL   What do I think?

KATIE   Would you come again?

MICHAEL   Would you like me to come again? (*Beat.*)
             Here.

KATIE   What's this?

MICHAEL   It's an address where you can reach me.

KATIE   About an hour from here? What's an hour from
             here? (*To audience.*) If I'd known then what
             we're starting to know now – from these books
             – and the letters in the newspapers – then
             perhaps . . . well . . . perhaps doesn't really
             come into it. Not when you've just met the man
             who's taken your little world, and turned it
             upside down, like a great big snowstorm in a
             picture jar. In my mind's eye I see it something
             like this . . .

*A kettle whistles. Lights slowly cross fade to a stark,
obviously freezing cold hut, with a curved, corrugated iron
ceiling. Also a table, a telephone and a blackboard. a young
woman – striking, unselfconscious – SHEILA ARBUTHNOT –
shouts at MICHAEL, now making a cup of coffee.*

SHEILA   You'll never make Fellow so long as you
             persist in drinking that beastly coffee at this
             hour of the afternoon. Do you want to hear a
             good one?

MICHAEL   What?

SHEILA   I heard this in the pub. Straight from the
             horse's mouth. Well, from the horse next to the
             horse's mouth. You'll love this.

MICHAEL   Why will I?

SHEILA   Because it reinforces one's fundamental sense
             of everything one holds dear about this

ridiculous bloody lovely little country. This
chap was telling me –

(MICHAEL *crosses. One mug of coffee, the other
of tea.*)

Nod's as good as a wink, etc, etc – one of the
code boys in Hut Six – apparently they had one
of these new whatsits in their hands. A brand
spanking new Heinkel with all the new
navigational equipment. Crash landed on the
beach at Swanage. What happens? Local army
boys get there first, waiting for the tide to go
out so they can drag it up the beach. Then the
Navy show. Senior bloody Service. A gunboat
off the beach. Assert their right to claim the
wreck, the wreck being between the high and
the low tide mark. Can you believe it?

MICHAEL   What do you mean, I'll never make Fellow?

SHEILA   The Navy end up *towing* the plane out to sea,
               where the rope breaks and the whole thing
               plunges into six fathoms of English Channel.

MICHAEL   (*handing her the tea*) Here.

               (*Beat.*)

SHEILA   So, what happened to our date?

MICHAEL   Date?

SHEILA   I was going to take you out. Remember?

MICHAEL   I've heard stories about you.

SHEILA   What stories?

MICHAEL   I've heard that instead of slowing down at
               junctions, you speed up. Is that true?

SHEILA   But of course it's true!

MICHAEL   But that's madness.

SHEILA   Are you aware of the statistical probability of
            hitting another car under wartime travel
            restrictions?

MICHAEL   Ah yes – I always forget. A linguist who is
            also a mathematician.

SHEILA   But here's the conundrum that's puzzling *me*.

MICHAEL   Yes?

SHEILA   A man goes home to his family for Friday Night
            Supper and comes back looking like he just
            scooped the bank at Monte Carlo.

            (MICHAEL *picks up a piece of paper. We see
            something projected onto a screen at the back
            of the stage. A jumble of words and figures:*)

STAB J 27 RETURN EVENING 19TH

STAB 2 AND 1, 19 AND 19

FIRST GRUPPE 41 AND 30, 52 AND 28

FOURTH GRUPPE 25 AND 10, 39 AND 18

**THEREOF IN OPERATIONAL AREA
FOREST.**

            (*Then, some words, incomplete, like a half-
            solved crossword clue:*)

MON**ICH S*****

            (MICHAEL *slides the piece of paper towards
            her.*)

MICHAEL   Are we missing something?

SHEILA   I am, certainly.

MICHAEL   I had a good weekend, thank you.

            (*Pause. The phone rings, a black bakelite
            phone on the table.* SHEILA *picks up the
            receiver, listens.*)

SHEILA   Yes. We're working on it. (*Beat.*) Work on it
            harder. (*Beat.*) Right-oh. (*She hangs up the
            phone.*) Jerry's the most literal-minded creature
            on the planet.

MICHAEL   You always say that.

SHEILA   Because it's true. I lived there.

MICHAEL   And I studied there.

SHEILA   I still can't believe they let a Jew Socialist from
            Birmingham study Schiller in Heidelberg.

MICHAEL   Where else would they let a Jew Socialist from
            Birmingham study Schiller? It was Schlegel
            anyway.

SHEILA   And who'd've thought you'd end up using it
            for this?

            (*A pause.*)

SHEILA   A name, at least?

MICHAEL   No name.

SHEILA   Why not?

MICHAEL   Because the less one thinks about a thing, the
            less likely that thing is to be buggered up.

SHEILA   I thought you were a romantic.

MICHAEL   I *am*. I am a romantic. That's the whole point.

SHEILA   The point of what?

MICHAEL   Romantic doesn't always mean happy endings,
               does it?

               (*Fade.*)

KATIE   (*to audience*) It was as if a curtain had been
               lifted on a whole glittering new world . . .

*As the scene changes, we hear the following, in the style of a
Pathe News commentary. Lights up on Bramble Street, where,
in due course,* KATIE *joins* JOANIE *in the sitting room,* JOANIE *at
the piano.*

MAN'S VOICE   (*excitable, 'clipped', upper class, voice*) 'Our
               Fighting services are striking hard at the
               enemy. Every man and woman in this country
               can and must help in the attack, must help to
               bring victory nearer. Here is something you can
               do. EMPLOYERS! If you are in the munitions
               industries be sure that each of your skilled men
               is employed up to the limit of his skill. Develop
               a training scheme in your works and prepare
               yourself now to take in new recruits –
               particularly women! If not engaged on work
               vital to the war effort, make it easy for your
               staff to volunteer for the Munitions Army.
               WOMEN . . . !'

WOMAN'S   'We're all helping on the kitchen front; making
VOICE   use of things which perhaps we shouldn't have
               bothered with in peace-time!' 'Yesterday, the
               Duchess of Gloucester was a guest of the Lord
               and Lady Mayoress of Coventry, where she
               was visiting the sick and injured at the
               Coventry and Warwickshire Hospital. Later,
               she showed off her cooking tips in the kitchen,
               teaching the nurses how to make a nourishing
               fish stew from the heads of fish!!

JOANIE   I still can't believe this is *you.*

KATIE   I agree it doesn't sound much like it. I'm
               standing there with five shillings. Five whole
               shillings pressed into my palm, thinking, I have
               to choose, I have to choose

JOANIE   Well obviously, it's no choice at all.

KATIE   In the middle of Owen Owen with a queue of
               old battle-axes lined up practically to the door,
               thinking, book or blouse, book or blouse . . .

JOANIE   When was the last time you bought anything at
               all for yourself?

KATIE   What's that you're playing?

JOANIE   This?

               (*She plays.*)

KATIE   You know I'm not very good with tunes.

               (*Plays a bit more.*)

JOANIE   (*croons jokily*) 'Twas like a breath of spring,
               heard a robin sing/About a nest set apart/All
               nature seemed to be in perfect harmony/Zing
               went the strings of my heart'.

KATIE   Is that supposed to be funny?

JOANIE   'Dear when you smiled at me, I heard a melody/
               It haunted me from the start . . .'

KATIE   Because I have to say, it isn't –

JOANIE   Anyway – you have to promise me.

KATIE   What?

JOANIE   *Next* time he comes, you don't keep him to
               yourself for the whole of the evening. And if
               Mr Oxford and Cambridge starts giving you airs

and graces, I'll show him something to prove
you're just as Coventry as the rest of us.

KATIE   What are you talking about?

JOANIE   We'll see what he thinks of you after he's seen
a photo of you in your pram on the beach at
Southport. With a great big snotgob hanging
from your nose.

KATIE   *Joanie –*

(*As* KATIE *play-chases her sister, she bumps
into* JACK, *who is entering followed by* MEG.)

What's the matter?

JACK   (*to* MEG) Why does it need a meeting? Because
a bunch of party lads have gone down, talk to
them there, how the shelters we've got are
useless. And while they're waiting, what
happens? Air raid. Try to make them leave.
Find a public shelter. Well bollocks to that.
We're going wherever you're going. So down
they go. Until they find themselves in a room.
A palace, a hundred feet underground. A
palace. Billiard Room, bar, beds. *You know
what I'm saying?*

MEG   *I* know what you're saying.

JACK   In the same week – the same bloody week –
we've got Bevin here, our own bloody Minister
of Labour telling us he knows us communists,
he knows what our problem is – we can't take it
– *that's our problem.* You could've heard a pin
drop in that room. A *pin.* That he'd *actually*
said it.

MEG   I just think . . . Jack . . . that you need to be
careful. They were arresting people like you, up
in Glasgow.

(KATIE *moves to the phone. Spot up on her,*
and on MICHAEL, *holding the bakelite phone*
receiver.)

MICHAEL   How come you've got a phone?

KATIE   Dad uses it for all his business.

MICHAEL   I thought he worked in a factory?

KATIE   Dad's Party, I told you.

MICHAEL   You talk about him all the time.

KATIE   I do not.

MICHAEL   I liked him.

            (*A slight pause.*)

KATIE   He got into a fight with his foreman.

MICHAEL   About what?

KATIE   Something about wages. Or shelters. I can
            never remember which.

MICHAEL   Do you find yourself arguing with him in your
            head?

KATIE   Yes! And sometimes –

MICHAEL   You end up doing it out loud –

KATIE   On a bus –

MICHAEL   Or in a lunch queue. I'm the same.

KATIE   Tell me about your family.

MICHAEL   They own a jewellery shop. In Birmingham.

KATIE   I should show you our watch.

MICHAEL   Watch?

KATIE   Our Grandad was famous for making watches. He made one once that cost *fifty pounds*.

MICHAEL   So what happened?

KATIE   He went bust, that's what happened. (*Beat.*) What do you argue with your father about?

MICHAEL   Everything. 'You dress like a goy. Why do you dress like a goy?' 'You talk like a goy?" What have they *done* to you at this Oxford University'.

KATIE   (*beat*) I expect he's very proud of you.

MICHAEL   I expect he is.

KATIE   What's a goy?

MICHAEL   Well, you are . . . sort of.

KATIE   I wish I could go there.

MICHAEL   You'd hate it.

KATIE   Would I? (*A slight pause.*) Tell me about your work.

MICHAEL   Katie . . .

KATIE   I know you can't talk about that. I mean your *real* work.

(MICHAEL *thinks*.)

MICHAEL   I came across something today. Made me think of you.'O selge, selge Nacht! Nur furcht ich, weil/Mich Nacht umgibt, dies alles sei nur Traum, Zu schmeichelnd suss, um wirklich zu bestehn.'

KATIE   What does it mean?

MICHAEL   There's a prize if you can guess what that is.

KATIE   Shakespeare, obviously. Hamlet? Julius
               Caesar?

MICHAEL   'O blessed, blessed night, I am afeard/Being in
               night, all this is but a dream/Too flattering
               sweet to be substantial.' (*Beat.*) You see, when
               the Germans translated him into their own
               language, they got rid of all the problems. A
               German reading Shakespeare understands
               Shakespeare far better than an English or a
               Scottish person. Which is why he's more
               important to them than he is to us. And I can't
               help thinking a people who claim Shakespeare
               as their own can't be *all* bad, can they?

KATIE   In spite of the things they're saying?

               (*Beat.*)

MICHAEL   That's not all Germans, Katie . . .

KATIE   (*beat*) When am I going to see you again?

MICHAEL   Soon.

KATIE   It's my birthday soon . . .

MICHAEL   I'll give you a call on the phone . . .

               (*Lights down.*)

A man appears in the Bletchley space: CAVE – *a man in his
mid-fifties wearing a tweed jacket with elbow patches.*

CAVE   In a way, I have more in common with them
               than I have with people here. The leading

scholars in my field are all German. That's just
the way it is.

I was talking to one of the other chaps here. He
told me he learned German in order to read the
German Expressionists. Now the German
Expressionists were bastard well over our
heads dropping bastard 500 pound bombs on
top of us.

So where did that leave things *now?*

(*As the lights come up on the main space at
Bletchley, the table is covered with reference
books and sheets of scribbles.* CAVE *withdraws
to the side. On the blackboard the previous
words are complete now.*)

MONDLICH SONATE

(*Accompanied by two others:*)

R*NS***RM   ***HEITSP****.**

SHEILA   There's something rather *chilling* about this, I
should say.

An operation, to be carried out, in ten days, at
the full moon. A performance, as it were.
Goering as conductor, the air force as
orchestra, like a ten finger exercise.

There's a separation of emotion and intellect at
work here wouldn't you say?

MICHAEL   Regenschirm.

(*He hefts a mighty dictionary and reads.*)

Brolly, gingham, umbrella, bumbershoot.
Bumbershoot. What the hell's a bumbershoot?

SHEILA   American, colloquial, for brolly.

MICHAEL   Gingham?

SHEILA   A type of material.

MICHAEL   This is the name of a place?

SHEILA   Can I ask you something?

MICHAEL   What?

SHEILA   Mr Sturm und Drang. Mr German Romantische.
               Have you ever actually *kissed* a girl?

MICHAEL   What? (*Beat.*) What kind of a question is that?
               You're obsessed.

SHEILA   Like Dr Freud.

MICHAEL   You read Sigmund Freud?

SHEILA   A girl likes to keep busy.

MICHAEL   My mother always said I should get analysed.

SHEILA   I shouldn't listen to her.

MICHAEL   I'm Jewish. I don't have any choice.

SHEILA   Personally – I don't believe in monsters in the
               attic.

MICHAEL   Why not?

SHEILA   If there's something in the attic, I go up there
               and I jolly well get rid of it.

MICHAEL   (*slightly puzzled*) Why are you telling me this?

SHEILA   Oh, I don't know . . .

               (*A long pause.* SHEILA *brings out a tennis ball.
               starts bouncing it up and down.*)

SHEILA   Last night, I was at the Duncombe Arms, in
            Sandy.

MICHAEL   They ought to keep a special place for you
            there.

            (*Beat.*)

SHEILA   I was talking to this chap. All alone at the bar.
            His brother was at sea. Merchant marine.
            Turned out he was in the convoy that was hit,
            off Newfoundland, on Saturday. I asked him
            what ship. He hesitated, but then he told me.
            And I knew at once that his brother was safe.
            That his brother was on one of the ships that
            came through.

MICHAEL   And?

SHEILA   And all I wanted to do was hold him. Reach out
            my arms, and hold him. Tell him it's okay. Your
            brother is okay. Now let's drink till the beer
            runs out of our eyes.

MICHAEL   And what did you say?

            (SHEILA *turns away. wipes a hand across the
            corner of her eye. Then.*)

SHEILA   Something terribly inappropriate, I should
            imagine. Or too clever for my own good . . .

            (*Fade. Lights up on Bramble Street.* KATIE
            enters the kitchen at the same time as JACK.)

KATIE   Dad?

JACK   Now what was it – I had something for you.

            (*He picks up a piece of paper – a letter – from
            the dresser.*)

Yes. (*He reads.*) Coventry Technical College. As you're still 'technically' a minor. And I'm still 'technically' your guardian. A letter, demanding to know . . . (*Reading.*) . . . that you have my 'full and complete support in this matter'. By which they mean, I imagine, I'm prepared to fork out for the books. And the clothes. What do you want for your birthday by the way?

KATIE   Is it okay if Michael comes to my birthday?

JACK   Michael? Who's Michael?

KATIE   You know.

JACK   Well, yes. I suppose. It won't be anything grand

KATIE   Why should he want anything grand?

JACK   You've spoken to him already then?

KATIE   No.

               (*Pause.*)

JACK   I'll send this back then shall I?

KATIE   Does it have to be today?

JACK   What's wrong with today? Are you coming selling papers with me later?

KATIE   I don't know . . .

JACK   Come on, it'll be a laugh. Then after, we'll go for a drink.

KATIE   Dad, what's litotes?

JACK   Litotes? Something medical by the sound of it.

KATIE   *Dad* . . . What's pathetic fallacy?

JACK   I don't know.

KATIE   What does philistine mean?

JACK   Philistine?

KATIE   You see, I didn't know, either.

JACK   So what?

KATIE   Dad, if I go and be a schoolteacher, now, what will *I* be able to tell children?

JACK   You?

KATIE   I've never *been* anywhere. I've never *done* anything. I've never *seen* anything.

JACK   You know a sight more than I do.

           (*Beat.*)

KATIE   Dad, I went to a lecture. Mr Gibson, the City Architect.

JACK   The one who wants to tear down Coventry and put a skyscraper up in its place?

KATIE   But you sit there, and you think, *how does he get an idea like that?* He said, if you were going to build a city, from scratch, *you wouldn't start with this, would you?*

JACK   This?

KATIE   Coventry. You wouldn't start with rotting buildings, stinking slums, factories in people's back gardens. You wouldn't start with that, would you?

JACK   I dare say you wouldn't. But I don't see it's for
                him, or for any one single person to tell us
                what's good for us and what isn't. Where's
                this all from, anyway?

KATIE   This?

                (*Lights up on a station platform. Different to
                the first one.* KATIE *quickly crosses into this
                space.*)

KATIE   You came!

MICHAEL   I kept thinking, what can be done in twenty-
                two minutes?

KATIE   (*holding a piece of paper up*) All Hail the
                Queen of the Timetable!

MICHAEL   And then I thought, a lot can be done in
                twenty-two minutes. (KATIE *pinches him.*)
                Ouch! What are you doing?

KATIE   I just want to be sure this is real.

MICHAEL   The world's fastest man can run five miles in
                twenty-two minutes. A man can listen to a
                whole Beethoven sonata in twenty-two
                minutes.

KATIE   Beethoven? What made you think of
                Beethoven?

MICHAEL   A lot can be done in twenty-two minutes.

KATIE   So let's stop talking about it, and let's *do* it.
                Here.

                (*She pushes a bag at him, which he opens.*)

MICHAEL   What's this?

KATIE   You said it was cold where you were. Gloves.

MICHAEL   You made these, for me?

KATIE   Did I stuff! Mum made them for me. But they
            don't fit.

MICHAEL   So what then?

KATIE   What?

MICHAEL   What shall we do?

KATIE   Seventeen minutes, and counting.

MICHAEL   We could have a cup of tea.

KATIE   Tea?

MICHAEL   Or a drink? What about a drink? I think there's
            a pub, across the road from here.

KATIE   You don't drink.

MICHAEL   I'm keen to learn.

KATIE   You said – Jews and alcohol don't mix.

MICHAEL   I can think of *one* thing . . .

KATIE   What? What?

            (*A slight pause.*)

MICHAEL   I like your dress.

KATIE   I thought you liked me in trousers.

MICHAEL   One doesn't preclude the other.

KATIE   I just want . . . I just wanted to be sure.

MICHAEL   What?

KATIE   That this . . . this is serious.

MICHAEL   *Serious*?

               (*Pause.*)

MICHAEL   We could go for a walk.

KATIE   You have to be honest. And not build me up.
               Into something I'm not.

MICHAEL   Why would I do that?

KATIE   Promise me.

MICHAEL   I promise you.

KATIE   It's funny. I listened to a play – a silly play on
               the radio. *Charley's Aunt.* I mean I *know* your
               life isn't like that.

MICHAEL   You'd be surprised.

KATIE   Michael, why won't you tell me what you do?

MICHAEL   Because, I can't

KATIE   I just . . . I want to know everything you know.
               I want to be everything you are. I want to go
               everywhere you go. I want to –

MICHAEL   Thirteen minutes.

KATIE   You wouldn't ever lie to me?

MICHAEL   Katie, why would I lie to you? Tell me. Under
               what circumstances would I *ever* lie to you?

               (*They lean towards each other. And kiss.
               Lights fade.*)

MICHAEL *crosses to the hut at Bletchley. As the lights come back up,* MICHAEL *and* SHEILA *are revealed playing a vigorous game of table hockey with a rubber and two books.*

MICHAEL   Regenschirm and Einheitspreis.

SHEILA   Regenschirm which makes us think of umbrella. Which makes us think of protection. Which makes us think of rain.

MICHAEL   Einheitspreis.

SHEILA   All one price.

MICHAEL   Which makes us think of . . .

SHEILA   Woolworths. Woolies. Wolverhampton.

MICHAEL   Why are we doing this?

SHEILA   It takes my mind off things.

MICHAEL   What things?

SHEILA   You know what I think?

MICHAEL   Most of the time, yes.

SHEILA   I think what a pal of mine thinks. (*Beat.*) A man was never truly attracted to a woman who he did not, in some respect, feel superior to.

MICHAEL   What do you mean?

SHEILA   What's your favourite book?

MICHAEL   *Hamlet*, of course.

SHEILA   Why?

MICHAEL   Because everything's in it. Love, doubt, life, choice – a man has to choose how to act. What about you?

SHEILA   *The Diary of a Nobody.*

MICHAEL   (*incredulous*) *The Diary of a Nobody*?

SHEILA   Because it's got everything in it. Love, doubt, life. But set in Peckham.

MICHAEL   That's so English.

SHEILA   But I am English. What a funny thing to say. Aren't *you* English?

                   (*Beat.*)

MICHAEL   Who's this pal of yours anyway?

SHEILA   Pal?

MICHAEL   The one you're always going on about?

SHEILA   His name's Greene. Another Greene. With an 'E'.

MICHAEL   The *writer?*

SHEILA   Yes, do you know him?

MICHAEL   What did you mean, I won't ever make Fellow?

                   (SHEILA *sits down at the piano in the corner. Absent-mindedly, she begins to pick out a piece of Beethoven.*)

SHEILA   You know what I hate most about this?

MICHAEL   Here?

SHEILA   At least, at boarding school, there actually *was* sex . . .

MICHAEL   At boarding school? And isn't there here?

SHEILA   Oh Michael . . . dear Michael . . . sometimes I
                wonder about you.

                (*Enter* CAVE. SHEILA *still playing.*)

CAVE   I hope I'm not interrupting anything?

                (SHEILA *stops.* MICHAEL *just stares at her. Beat.*
                CAVE *crosses to the blackboard and stands,*
                like an old-fashioned schoolmaster.)

                (*to recap*) In early November, it was reported
                by a Prisoner of War, in conversation with a
                room mate, that a raid was planned, to take
                place between the 15th and the 20th of
                November, at the full moon.

                On the 12th, Airforce Intelligence was able to
                amplify this information sufficiently to confirm
                that a heavy scale raid was probable during
                this time: that the Knickebein and VHF beams
                would be employed; that Air Fleets 2 and 3,
                together with KG-100, amounting to over 1800
                front line aircraft, would be participating.

MICHAEL   (*almost to himself*) 'Proud of their numbers and
                secure in soul . . .'

CAVE   There were two target names cropping up as
                alternatives. Regenschirm and Einheitpreis.

                There is now a third beginning to appear.

                (CAVE *chalks the word* **'KORN'**, *slowly and*
                deliberately on the blackboard.)

                (*beat*) The word we're receiving is that Hitler is
                upset about Munich. He's fed up with the way
                the war is going and he wishes to make a very
                big statement. He intends to hit ordinary
                workers' dwellings as well as factories. The
                belief, in Germany, being that morale amongst
                the working classes is close to breaking.

SHEILA   And is it?

CAVE   Is it what?

MICHAEL   Is it close to breaking?

CAVE   (*beat*) You're asking the wrong chap there, I'm
              afraid.

SHEILA   I thought you spent quite a lot of time at the
              swimming baths, sir.

CAVE   The swimming baths?

SHEILA   Yes sir. I thought, perhaps, on one of your
              trips . . . to the swimming baths . . . you might
              have picked something up.

              (*Beat.*)

CAVE   (*ignoring this*) You're a Queens' Oxford man
              aren't you Green?

MICHAEL   Yes Sir.

CAVE   I'm having dinner with your college President
              tomorrow night.

MICHAEL   Sir?

CAVE   Green's a Jewish name, isn't it?

MICHAEL   Yes sir.

CAVE   Greenberg, or something like that, it would
              have been originally. (*Beat.*) Well, I'll send him
              your regards, shall I?

              (*Exit* CAVE.)

SHEILA   Michael?

MICHAEL   Yes?

SHEILA   I've had the most wonderful idea.

MICHAEL   Yes?

SHEILA   Why don't you take me home with you?

MICHAEL   Home?

SHEILA   To Birmingham. I'd most awfully like to see it. I could drive. We could go down together . . .

MICHAEL   You've never been to *Birmingham*?

SHEILA   *No.* Wouldn't that be fun?

                (*Lights fade.*)

JOHN MARTIN *now walks to the front of the stage again. We are back, briefly, in 1976.*

MARTIN   (*as if still speaking to* KATIE) You ask if my memory is clear? If the facts relating to that day remain clear and fresh in my mind? I tell you that they do.

                (*A moment.*)

                The diary was my sole responsibility. Nothing was entered, nothing was taken out, without my express say-so. And I should add: I knew the man by then about as well as a man can know another man.

                That week in particular? Our ships had won a great battle, against the Italians, at Taranto. And Chamberlain was buried, at Westminster. So yes, I remember that week.

                (*Slow fade. Lights up on* MICHAEL *and* KATIE *holding their respective phone receivers.*)

KATIE   What's German for: 'Dost thou love me? I know
               thou will say Ay/And I will take thy word: yet,
               if thou swear'st/ Thou mayst prove false: at
               lovers' perjuries/They say Jove laughs.'

MICHAEL   Are you serious?

KATIE   Has poetry ever stopped, or started a war, do
               you think?

MICHAEL   It's never stopped one. But I'm pretty sure it
               must have started one.

KATIE   You can still come to my birthday, can't you?

MICHAEL   I hope so.

KATIE   Are the girls where you are pretty Michael?

MICHAEL   Pretty? No, they're not pretty. Nothing about
               this place is pretty.

               (*Lights fade.*)

*The hut. The '**KORN**' transcript remains visible behind them.*
SHEILA *seems pre-occupied.*

MICHAEL   Korn.

SHEILA   (*grave*) Yes.

MICHAEL   Another word for corn.

SHEILA   Chaff.

MICHAEL   Chaff's American for noise, chatter.

SHEILA   Meaning distortion.

MICHAEL   Perhaps referring to our attempts to block out
               the beams . . .

SHEILA   Perhaps.

MICHAEL   Korn. Just meaning corn.

SHEILA   Meaning countryside.

MICHAEL   Why would they be interested in the
                countryside?

SHEILA   (*preoccupied*) Everyone's interested in our
                countryside. It's interesting.

MICHAEL   It probably isn't even a place. (*Thinking
                aloud.*) Korn's the name of a spirit. Grain spirit.
                Whisky. What about Churchill? Churchill
                drinks whisky. Or Scotland!

SHEILA   They can't reach Scotland . . .

MICHAEL   Of course they can reach Scotland. How would
                you know, anyway? You've probably never
                even *been* there . . .

                (*Pause.*)

MICHAEL   What did you mean, I'll never make Fellow?

                (*Suddenly, without warning,* SHEILA *takes*
                MICHAEL'S *head and tries to kiss him.* MICHAEL
                *is so shocked, he doesn't know how to
                respond.*)

                (*Pause.*)

SHEILA   Michael, you do realise, we could both be here
                for the next ten years of our lives?

                (*They consider this awful prospect for a
                moment.*)

                Look, in an ideal world, I'd be driving
                ambulances in Africa.

MICHAEL   (*still astonished*) So why don't you?

SHEILA   For the same reason *you* don't. (*Long pause.*)
            This place depends for its existence on a
            supply of oddballs like you and me.

MICHAEL   I'm not an oddball.

SHEILA   Solipsistic, emotionally constipated cranks
            with egg in their beards and their trousers
            tucked into their socks.

MICHAEL   I'm not a crank.

SHEILA   (*trembling*) Look, there are times when I hardly
            know how I'm going to make it to the end of
            the *day*, let alone the end of the war. When I
            feel like taking off all my clothes and running
            naked through the High Street in Dunstable.

MICHAEL   So why don't you?

            (SHEILA *is almost shaking, then seems to stop,
            think for a moment, and frown. Slowly she
            crosses to the table, picks up a fat volume: a
            German edition of the Complete Works of
            Shakespeare. Opens it and flicks through.*)

MICHAEL   (*puzzled*) What are you doing?

            (SHEILA *checks something, and absorbs the
            implications.*)

SHEILA   (*at length*) I think we've both been rather dim,
            Michael.

MICHAEL   How have we?

SHEILA   (*taking a moment*) Do you remember a book?
            Arthur Mee's *500 Extraordinary Facts and
            Amazing Figures*. It was my absolutely
            favourite book as a child: jokes, tricks, quiz
            questions.

MICHAEL   Quiz questions?

SHEILA   Oh, you know, things like . . . (*She thinks.*) 'In
               what year was the last wolf captured in
               England?' 'In which battle did a King of
               England last lead the assault?' And this one, I
               don't know why I always remember this one.
               'Which is the only named character in
               Shakespeare to appear and *not to speak a
               line*?'

               (*She hands the relevant passage to* MICHAEL.)

               This is your big thing I thought – Shakespeare,
               translated into German?

MICHAEL   (*reads*) 'Auftritt Warwick, Bürgermeister von
               Koventry.'

               (MICHAEL *absorbs this, stares into the
               distance.*)

MICHAEL   Why didn't you say before?

SHEILA   Because it's only just occurred to me.

MICHAEL   You're saying Korn is Coventry?

SHEILA   Yes.

               (MICHAEL *is horror-struck.*)

               Michael what's the matter?

               (MICHAEL *doesn't reply.* SHEILA *frowns,
               beginning to absorb the implications. Slow
               fade.*)

Bramble Street. There is a sound. JACK, *covered in oil, enters
through the front door.* MEG *waits for him.*

MEG   So that's all fixed then is it?

JACK   (*holding up a carbonised spark plug*) Not
           much to look at, is it? But without it, car
           doesn't run.

MEG   Even for you?

JACK   Like a craftshop without a craftsman. You don't
           miss him till he's gone.

MEG   Not much danger of them not missing you, is
           there? Jack . . .

JACK   What . . .

           (*Pause.*)

MEG   Why are you so dead set on going to my
           sister's tomorrow?

JACK   Why? Because I'm off work, it's a full moon, it
           makes no *sense* to stay – does it?

           (*Pause.*)

MEG   You know she's thought of nothing else but
           this, for days.

           (*Beat. singing is heard, off.* JACK *bites his lip.*)

JOANIE   (*off*) 'Who's gonna take you home tonight/
           Take your hand and hold you tight/Who'll be
           the one to make it right/ And promise you
           paradise . . .'

           (JOANIE *enters.*)

JACK   I don't want you singing that one.

JOANIE   Why not?

JACK   Because it's mucky.

MEG   You're early.

JOANIE   We were finished by two o'clock. Half the
               people never showed up.

JACK   (*to* MEG) See?

JOANIE   Half of them've left already, trekking. So. I've
               just time to drop this off –

JACK   What?

JOANIE   (*produces something from her bag with a
               flourish*) This is what you asked for, isn't it?

               (JACK *takes it. A book – 'Palgrave's First
               Treasury of poems.' Clearly a book aimed at a
               child.*)

JOANIE   Oh, and I almost forgot.

               (JOANIE *pulls something else from her bag,
               which she throws down on the table. A carton
               of cigarettes.*)

MEG   What's this?

               (JACK *doesn't answer.*)

JOANIE   Aren't you going to ask me where I got them?

JACK   I don't have to ask do I? Netty Harper.

JOANIE   Who are they for?

JACK   Never you mind.

               (MEG *turns her back and goes off.*)

JOANIE   Netty was asking about Vi's. When were we
               going there.

JACK   Why is she asking that?

JOANIE   I told her not tomorrow at any rate. We were
              having a party, here.

              (*Children's singing from outside – 'The Big
              Ship Sails in the Alley Alley-oh', etc, etc.
              Pause.*)

JOANIE   Dad. Someone told me, at Liverpool, the other
              night, they just did what they wanted. No
              guns, no fighters, nothing. Just walked in, nice
              as you like. Like shooting fish in a barrel. The
              government wouldn't let that happen here,
              would they?

              (*Lights fade.*)

Outside, at Bletchley. Enter CAVE, *dressed for a journey.*
MICHAEL, *breathless, catches him.*

MICHAEL   (*breathless*) Sir? Sir?

CAVE   Green. What is it?

              (MICHAEL *pants, uncontrollably.*)

CAVE   Your thing's the Middle Ages isn't it?

MICHAEL   What sir?

CAVE   Just checking. Want to be sure I know what I'm
              talking about with Malcolm . . .

              (*A slight pause.* MICHAEL *almost has his breath
              back now.*)

MICHAEL   Sir, I know what Moonlight Sonata is.

CAVE   What?

MICHAEL   Korn, sir. We've been all round the houses.
              Sheila Arbuthnot's always banging on. The

Germans are the most literal-minded creatures on the planet. But in this case she's absolutely right.

CAVE   What are you on about?

MICHAEL   This, sir.

CAVE   (*he looks at the book*) What's this?

MICHAEL   It's obvious sir. It's been staring us in the bloody face.

                (*A slight breath. On the screen behind, a page of German text – a play – is now projected. A page of Shakespeare, in German. with the already-quoted line clearly picked out:* **'Auftritt Warwick, Bürgermeister von Koventry, zwei Boten und andere, oben auf der Mauer.'**)

MICHAEL   This is what I do sir. Translations of Shakespeare. Schlegel. And Tieck.

CAVE   You're blathering.

MICHAEL   The battle scene, at the end of the third part of Henry the Sixth. The stage direction, sir.

CAVE   (*reads*) Auftritt Warwick, Bürgermeister von Koventry, zwei Boten und andere, oben auf der Mauer.

MICHAEL   (*translating*) 'Enter Warwick, the Mayor of Coventry, two messengers and others upon the walls.' Coventry, sir. The Germans spell Coventry with a K.

CAVE   Meaning?

MICHAEL   The codes don't need to be very complicated. *Because no one's supposed to be reading them.*

CAVE   You're saying Korn is Coventry?

MICHAEL   Yes sir.

CAVE   But it could be anywhere. Anywhere beginning
                with a C . . . or a K.

MICHAEL   Such as? (CAVE *doesn't reply.*) Kettering?
                Caversham? Kidderminster? Why would
                anyone send 1800 bombers to bomb
                Kidderminster?

CAVE   Good work, Green.

MICHAEL   Sir?

CAVE   Very clever.

MICHAEL   This'll go straight to the top – won't it?

CAVE   Oh, I expect so.

MICHAEL   You expect so?

                (*A moment.*)

CAVE   You know, Wordsworth called Coventry . . . the
                most beautiful of all English cities.

                (*Beat.*)

                A great pity. Yes. A great, great pity.

                (*Lights fade.*)

It's 1976. JOHN MARTIN *again steps forward.*

MARTIN   (*as if speaking to* KATIE) When there was
                knowledge of routine raids Churchill and I
                would travel up to Ditchley, in Oxfordshire.

There we would eat, sleep, talk and watch films, projected onto the wall in the library.

The signals would arrive each day from Broadway, a yellow box, which I would hand to him in his office, or if we were travelling somewhere, in the car on the way.

(MICHAEL *and* KATIE *cross to their respective phones, pick up the receivers. We're back in 1940.*)

KATIE   (*gushing*) So. Mum's going to do her hotpot. And Joanie's going to sing. And then . . . and then . . . we're free! Free to do whatever we want. Go for a walk. Go to the pictures. It's *The Wizard of Oz*. Would you like to see *The Wizard of Oz*, Michael?

(MICHAEL *just stares into space. Lights down.*)

Lights slowly up on Bramble Street. We are aware – for the first time – of the space at the back of the yard. a wooden structure – steps leading up to some kind of platform, invisible and offstage – straddles the fence separating the yard from the alley.

KEN descends slowly into view, peering upwards at the sky through a pair of service binoculars. JOANIE appears in the alley, holding a thermos flask.

The sound of a single twin-engined aircraft is heard soaring in the sky above.

JOANIE   I brought this for you.

KEN   Look at that!

JOANIE   I am looking at that.

KEN

What the bloomin' heck does he think he's
playing at?

JOANIE

Looks like a great big question mark, in the sky.
What do they call that?

KEN

Vapour trail. You know it's not one of ours,
don't you?

JOANIE

You look so cold, perched up there.

(JOANIE *hands* KEN *the flask. He pauses for a
second before taking it.*)

What do you think he means by that question
mark?

(*The crisp November air is broken by the
crackle of a service band radio, unintelligible
prattle.*)

(*almost to herself*) Question mark over
Coventry. Sounds like a book, doesn't it?

Don't you get lonely, up there?

KEN

Lonely? Why should I get lonely? (*He stamps
his feet on the ground, as if to get warm.*) All
human life is here, I'm telling you. There's a
man down Vecqueray Street, spends all his time
in the attic. I reckon he's got a radio in there.
And that lady, lives above the greengrocers in
Gosford Street. You don't even want to know
what goes on up there . . . And that funny
bloke, in Charterhouse Street.

JOANIE

I heard he joined your lot.

KEN

Ha ha.

JOANIE

I'm serious.

KEN

You watch your step young lady.

(*Suddenly, we hear a child's voice in the
alley. A boy of eight or nine.*)

'I love coffee/I love tea/I love the girls and the
girls love me.'

(*Then a couple of girlish giggles.*)

Cross fade with the house. JACK *on his own. He goes up to the
window, looks out. Enter* KATIE *through the front door. She
comes and stands behind him.*

KATIE   Have you been outside?

JACK   Katie . . .

KATIE   Not even dark yet. Look at the size of that
            moon. Look – you can see the Sea of
            Tranquility. (*Beat.*) Dad, why won't you even
            talk to me?

JACK   About what?

KATIE   About what I was asking you.

JACK   Katie, I've said all I've got to say on the topic
            of university. If you're that concerned about
            the future of this place, we've got more than
            enough colleges here. We've the best
            Technical College in the country, practically . . .

            (*Enter* MEG. KATIE *suddenly spots the
            cigarettes.*)

KATIE   These are Auntie Vi's, aren't they? The ones
            she smokes?

            (*Beat.*)

MEG   Come over here. Help me with the spuds.

(JACK *moves away. Pause.*)

MEG   Tell me again what you've arranged?

KATIE   (*beat*) He phoned me. (*Finding the envelope.*)
            What's this?

MEG   A letter. Come for you.

            (KATIE *rips it open in excitement. Her face
            lights up, as she reads the typewritten letter
            inside.*)

            What is it?

KATIE   Nothing.

MEG   A letter comes for you, from Oxford, and you
            can't tell us what's in it? (KATIE *doesn't
            answer.*) What did he say? That he was
            coming?

KATIE   (*beat*) Yes. That he was coming . . . (*Beat.
            Almost beside herself with excitement.*) Mum. I
            never told you about how we met.

MEG   You didn't.

KATIE   If you knew that, you wouldn't be like this.

MEG   We don't know anything, that's the difficulty.

KATIE   We talk every day on the phone. He calls me
            his Rosalind.

MEG   Rosalind?

KATIE   Because Rosalind is in *As You Like It*, and I
            was going to Henley to do gardening for
            Auntie Vi when the siren went.

MEG   You've lost me girl.

KATIE   Rosalind dressed as a boy. In the Forest of
             Arden.

MEG   You better just come and help me . . .

KATIE   What's the matter? What's the matter?

             (KATIE, *in a world of her own, goes through to
             the kitchen, while* MEG *goes to speak to* JACK,
             who stands holding KATIE'S *present – the book
             – and a pair of scissors*.)

MEG   You're going to have to make up your mind.

             (MEG *begins to busy herself in the 'shelter'
             area beneath the stairs. Picking up things left
             there from last time. A thermos, and some
             mugs*.)

MEG   Someone has to decide one way or the other.
             (*She carries an obviously brimming chamber
             pot to the back door*) If we're staying, then I
             need to get cooking, and someone needs to get
             to the shop.

JACK   What for?

             (*Unseen by either of them,* KATIE *returns, puts
             the letter down and begins to take off her
             shoes*.)

MEG   Look I don't care where, or what, or how. But
             in case you hadn't noticed we're supposed to
             be celebrating something this evening, and
             we're not going to celebrate with bloody barley
             water.

             (JACK *turns round and sees* KATIE.)

JACK   (*looking down*) Katie, how come you're taking
             your shoes off?

KATIE   I can take off my shoes, can't I?

JACK   Katie –

KATIE   What?

JACK   You need to get ready.

KATIE   Only to go to the shop.

JACK   No one needs to go to the shop.

KATIE   You've just heard Mum, haven't you? What if
            people want to drink beer? What if Mum wants
            some?

            (JACK *turns to* MEG.)

JACK   Mum?

MEG   Look, don't involve me.

JACK   (*incredulous*) You've never drunk beer in your
            life. Why would you suddenly start tonight?

KATIE   There's other people to be considered.

JACK   Other people?

KATIE   (*beat*) What if Ken wants some?

JACK   Ken?

KATIE   Or Michael . . .

JACK   (*beat*) But love . . .

KATIE   (*puts shoes back on*) I'll get to the outdoor.
            Another bottle of Mann's for Dad, and half a
            dozen of Ansell's for whoever.

            (*Beat.*)

JACK   Katie – we're going to Henley.

KATIE   Who is?

JACK   We all are.

KATIE   What are you talking about? (*Pause.
            stunned.*) Dad – Michael's coming . . . (*Pause.*)

JACK   (*gently*) I got this for you. (*He hands her the
            book.*) Haven't had time to wrap it up. It's what
            you wanted – isn't it?

            (*She looks at it. He's made an effort, but it's
            obviously not.*)

KATIE   Dad – you'll get to like him.

JACK   He's a chap you met at a railway station.

KATIE   Not just a chap. He's a Lecturer in Literature.
            At Oxford University.

JACK   Ah – Oxford University.

            (*Pause.*)

KATIE   Dad, we were caught by the siren. He saw me
            all the way to the front door. He's written to me
            every day.

            (*Silence.*)

JACK   So what does he do then, this Michael?

KATIE   Translating.

JACK   Maybe something wrong with his health.

KATIE   There's nothing wrong with his health.

JACK   It just seems odd, that's all.

KATIE   Odd? Why odd?

JACK   It just seems odd from where I'm sitting –

KATIE   He's not allowed to talk about it.

JACK   Why not?

KATIE   Look I don't know why not. Why don't you ask
                him? Tonight? (*Pause.*) Each according to their
                ability. Isn't that what you say? What about
                your precious Bevin – the Bevin boys.

JACK   He's not my precious Bevin. Not since he gave
                that speech here. 'I know you Harry Pollitt. I
                know you communists. You can't take it, and
                that's your problem.'

KATIE   Well, maybe he's got a point.

JACK   What did you say? (*Suddenly furious.*) What
                did you say?

                (KATIE *rushes out of the house, leaving her
                stunned father rooted to the spot.*)

MEG   Now look what you've done. *Now look what
                you've done.*

                (*Lights slowly fade.*)

MICHAEL *finally picks up the receiver. He begins to dial. at
Bramble Street. The phone rings out twice. At the wall,* SHEILA
pulls the cord from the socket.

SHEILA   What are you doing?

MICHAEL   (*turning*) Put it back.

SHEILA   No.

MICHAEL   Put it back.

SHEILA   If necessary, I'll scream.

MICHAEL   Scream? Put it back.

SHEILA   No, Michael.

                (*He approaches her. Grabs the cord.*)

                Give it back.

MICHAEL   Why?

SHEILA   Because – you *know* why.

                (*A stand off.*)

                You need some rest.

MICHAEL   You said it yourself – when you were talking to
                that man in the bar. *You wanted to tell him.*

SHEILA   I wanted to. Yes. But I didn't. The signal's
                gone up. Measures will be taken.

MICHAEL   *We're talking about the biggest single raid,
                outside London, since Guernica.*

SHEILA   Rien a faire.

MICHAEL   What?

SHEILA   Rien a faire. We're going to the pub. Dilly Knox
                is taking us to the pub. Why don't you come
                Michael? Why don't you come?

                (*He makes to plug the cord back in.*)

                I promise you, I will scream.

MICHAEL   And say *what*?

SHEILA   That I have reason to believe you've taken
                leave of your senses.

MICHAEL	At the very least I must phone, tell them I'm *not* coming.
SHEILA	Giving what excuse? Michael . . . you're one of the very worst liars in the history of creation.
MICHAEL	And if it was *your* father, or *your* mother?
SHEILA	I don't have a father or a mother.
MICHAEL	Your town?
SHEILA	I hardly think the Germans are going to bomb Winchester now are they?
	(MICHAEL *makes a sudden further movement to re-plug the cord.*)
	Give it to me. Give it to me. Give it to me.
	(*He slumps down in a chair. Thinks for a moment, then hands her the cord.*)
	(*reassuring*) There'll be air cover. Balloons. Most of their planes won't even reach the target. Courage, mon brave. Courage . . .
	(*Lights fade.*)

Lights up on Bramble Street, a little later. The table is laid for a birthday tea – cake, sandwiches, etc. But KATIE'S *absence is almost palpable.* JACK *stands mutely apart.* KEN *suddenly produces something from inside his coat. what looks like a human hand.*

JOANIE	(*shriek*) What's that?
	(*She screams.*)
KEN	Had you going, didn't it?

JOANIE   What is it?

KEN   From the dress shop. In Gosford Street.

JOANIE   That's awful.

KEN   I'll tell you what's awful. Couple of lads nicked
           in Gulson Road for gambling in a shelter.
           That's what's awful. What right have men in
           London got telling lads what they can and
           can't do in shelters. I bet that fat bastard
           Churchill doesn't stop playing bridge when the
           bombs start to fall. (*A slight pause.*) Maybe I
           should pop back later?

           (*A tear runs down* MEG'S *face.*)

           Where d'you reckon she can have got to?

MEG   We've no idea. That's the problem.

           (*A slight pause, then* KEN *gets up to go.*)

           Where are you headed now?

KEN   The base, in Terry Road.

MEG   Will you keep an eye out?

KEN   Of course I will. (*Pause.*) And remember –
           whatever you decide – chalk it up on the door.

           (KEN *goes. Silence. Outside, we hear the
           sounds of children playing:
           neeeeeeeeeooooow. Aircraft noises. In a daze,*
           JOANIE *wanders out into the yard. Awkward
           silence.*)

JOANIE   (*from outside*) It's true what they say you
           know, you *can* read the newspaper. It's that
           bright.

(JOANIE *holds up a copy of the Telegraph – left there earlier by* JACK.)

JOANIE   (*shouting out headlines*) "Colds prevented by vitamin C." "Gracie gets a medal." "Film star learns to fly." Well *that's* alright then, isn't it?

(*Suddenly, there is the unmistakeable low rumble of aircraft engines in the distance. And, a split-second later, the sound of an air-raid siren.*)

MEG   (*coming to the door*) Joanie, get in here, now.

(*But* JOANIE *is fixed to the spot. Her parents are drawn, as if by a force beyond their power, into the yard. the sound is distant at first – the first suggestion of a rumble. Then clearer. The sound of aircraft engines. Rumbling closer, and closer and closer. At a distance we hear the unmistakeable sound of an explosion.*)

MEG   (*retreating inside to prepare the shelter*) Joanie – get in here now!

JOANIE   It's alright. Dad said it was alright.

MEG   Dad?

JOANIE   Because they're not aiming at us are they?

MEG   Joanie!

JOANIE   The Germans aren't the real enemy, they're not interested in people like us, only factories and railways and such-like . . . they're socialists.

MEG   They're the wrong sort of socialists.

JOANIE   Dad said the German working man isn't interested in harming his fellow workers, only in smashing the machinery of capitalism. And as soon as they've done that, they'll smash the Nazis, too.

MEG   Joanie – for Christ's sake.

               (JACK *and* MEG *begin feverishly to load the shelter. All of a sudden, there is a deafening whine, followed by an explosion, and the stage is plunged into darkness.*)

JOANIE   Jesus Christ . . . !!

               (*Interval.*)

ACT TWO

Spot on JOHN MARTIN. *It is 1976.*

MARTIN   (*as if addressing* KATIE) Having opened the box, Churchill immediately instructed the driver to turn round and go back to Downing Street. He explained that the navigation beams were intersecting over London, indicating a heavy raid, and *he was not going to spend the night peacefully in the country while the metropolis was under heavy attack.*

        Did I see the contents of the box? The actual, physical contents of the box? (*Long pause.*) No, I did not. (*An admission.*) The Prime Minister was the only person to do so.

        We were expecting the most massive of bombardments. I myself accompanied him to the Air Ministry roof, where we drank champagne and smoked Havana cigars, in anticipation of the raid to come.

Spot fades on MARTIN. *Back to 1940.* SHEILA *joins* CAVE *on the lawn in front of Bletchley Park.* CAVE *looks upwards at the sky. The drone of bombers is audible above.*

CAVE   (*an imitation*) "I will inform you at six each evening at which office I shall dine, work and sleep. Accommodation will be required for Mrs C, two shorthand writers, three secretaries and Nelson the cat. There shall be shelter for all, and a place for me to watch air raids from the roof."

        (*A slight pause.*)

CAVE   A little bird tells me Green has a connection in Coventry.

SHEILA	Yes sir.
CAVE	It wouldn't occur to him to do anything stupid would it?
SHEILA	Stupid, sir? No sir. I don't think so.
CAVE	Awfully bad luck about your car.
SHEILA	Yes sir.
CAVE	You don't have any idea what can have happened to it do you?
SHEILA	No sir.
CAVE	(*deliberate*) I think it's probably worth saying at this point that the penalty for treason is still the same, you know . . .

(*The noise of the bombers intensifies. Cross fade with:*)

Lights dimly up on an indeterminate space. Outside, a low crump of bombs falling. A body lies on the ground. Next to the body are other shapes, also indeterminate. There is movement. The "body" wakes with a start, fighting for breath.

PETER *enters, wearing a grey jumper and ecclesiastical dog collar – carrying a cup of tea.*

KATIE	(*as if in a dream*) Where am I?
PETER	You're safe here.
KATIE	(*total disorientation*) I thought . . .
PETER	. . . in the dark . . .
KATIE	I thought . . . (*Coming to.*) coloured lights . . .

PETER   Here.

KATIE   What is it?

PETER   Hot sweet tea. You'll feel right again in a
             minute.

KATIE   Where am I?

PETER   You're okay here. Just rest for a minute.

             (*Pause.*)

KATIE   I was riding . . .

PETER   You were outside.

KATIE   (*fighting to remember*) Towards the station. I
             was riding towards the station. Someone
             yanked me off.

             (*Beat.*)

             My bike. I ran back to pick it up. A soldier said
             there's a big shelter up at Owen's. I gave this
             girl a croggy up Hertford Street. When we got
             there, it was burning.

             (*Pause.*)

PETER   Croggy.

KATIE   What?

PETER   It's funny.

KATIE   Why funny?

PETER   (*beat*) I was ten years away from Coventry. I
             didn't even realise we *had* an accent.

KATIE   We?

(KATIE *is confused.*)

KATIE   Where am I?

PETER   Don't you recognise it?

KATIE   (*dazed*) I can't see properly.

PETER   You don't remember anything?

KATIE   No.

PETER   (*he smiles*) High explosive. In Bayley Lane.
             Must've blown you right off your feet.
             Someone brought you in.

KATIE   The girl on the bike?

PETER   A policeman.

KATIE   What happened to the girl on the bike?

             (PETER *doesn't reply.*)

             Where am I?

PETER   Probably the safest place in Coventry right at
             the moment.

KATIE   I have to go.

PETER   You've had a very nasty bump.

KATIE   I have to get to the station.

             (*She tries to leave but* PETER *bars her way.*)

             (*wildly*) You don't understand. Michael's
             coming. *Michael's* coming . . .

             (*Cross fade with:*)

In the darkness, the relentless drone of the bombers.

Lights up on the shelter area at Bramble Street. Bombs falling in the middle distance.

A Monopoly board is visible on the floor. The house is suffused with an eery, phosphorescent glow.

MEG	Hat, shoe?
JOANIE	I don't mind.
MEG	Dad?
JACK	Iron then.
MEG	You can't be the iron.
JACK	Why not?
MEG	Joanie?
JOANIE	I don't care. Ship.
MEG	Or the ship.
JOANIE	Why not? Mum?
	(*Beat.*)
MEG	We should play Coventry rules.
JACK	What?
	(JOANIE *gets up, out of the shelter, and goes to the kitchen window. Gazes in wonder. The glow increases in intensity.*)
MEG	Joanie . . .
JOANIE	It's alright, it's easing off a bit. (*Beat.*) Like Pinnochio.

MEG   Pinnochio?

JOANIE   When The Green Fairy appears. Lights up
              everything around her. I've never seen
              anything like it.

              (*A series of blasts, like fireworks.*)

MEG   (*remembering*) That time in Wales. Remember?

              (*Pause.*)

              You said you'd only play if we changed the
              names from bloody London. Walsgrave Road,
              Gulson Road, Cash's Lane.

              (*Pause.*)

MEG   (*quietly*) I was the iron. Dad'd be the car. And
              Katie'd be the ship.

              (*Silence. The tears roll down* MEG'S *cheek.*)

JACK   For Christ's sake . . . what's happened to the
              bloody guns?

              (*Pause.*)

JOANIE   Do you want to hear something funny?

MEG   That'd be nice, dear.

JOANIE   You know them big ack-ack lorries they been
              driving in and out of town, through the streets
              and everything?

MEG   Yes.

JOANIE   You know how we've all been saying, we shall
              be alright with them looking after us?

JACK   What about them?

(*Beat.*)

JOANIE   There's only one of them.

JACK   What do you mean, there's only one of them?

            (*Pause.*)

JOANIE   (*hesitant*) This lad – a friend of somebody's, he
            told me – the others are all away, defending
            other cities. So they've just got the one.

JACK   How does he know?

JOANIE   Because it's his job to drive it, in and out of
            the city, by a different route every day.

JACK   How come you're meeting lads?

JOANIE   He said he'd go to prison if anyone found out.

            (JACK *lost in thought for a moment.*)

MEG   (*at length*) If she could have phoned, she
            would have done, wouldn't she?

            (*Long pause.*)

MEG   Joanie, what about a song?

            Come on, a song – what about Ten Green
            Bottles. Or She'll be Coming Round the
            Mountain.

JOANIE   Mum . . .

JACK   No sign of Wonderboy, at any rate.

MEG   Wonderboy?

JACK   All day sharpening their pencils, wearing the
            arses out of their trousers. Then the minute a

dog so much as farts outside in the street, a
nice concrete-reinforced bunker to climb into.

MEG   (*angry*) How can you say that? How can you
           say that?

           (JOANIE *starts to hum, and then to sing.*)

JOANIE   'She'll be coming round the mountain when she
           comes/She'll be coming round the mountain
           when she comes/She'll be wearing pink
           suspenders, bloomers and pajamas/And a pair
           of frilly knickers on her bum.'

MEG   Why hasn't she phoned?

JACK   The line's probably down.

MEG   What if it isn't?

JACK   We should try and get some sleep.

           Here . . . we could try the curtain – pull it
           across . . .

           (JACK *pulls a curtain across the shelter area,
           masking the three family members from view. A
           series of enormous explosions. Lights fade.*)

A police barrier.

A woman in a hat – HILDE CHAMBERS (*actor playing* SHEILA) *–
approaches the* SPECIAL CONSTABLE (*actor playing* CAVE)
posted at the barrier.

From behind, and in the dark, HILDE *looks at first a little like*
KATIE.

*The stage is suffused by a red glow. During the following, we
become aware of a sound, initially unclear to us, but
increasingly loud and insistent . . .*

OFFICER   No way through missus.

HILDE   Press –

OFFICER   I don't care if you're Princess bloody Elizabeth,
               there's no way through.

HILDE   I was in Birmingham. Someone said –'we're fed
               up hearing about London – come and tell your
               readers about us.' I was sitting in the grill room
               at the Midland when a man came in. 'I've just
               come from Coventry, he says, with a lorry, and
               they aren't half copping it bad'.

OFFICER   We've got fire crews coming from Birmingham,
               Leicester, Stafford – all over the bloody
               Midlands – I can't afford to let that cab in here.

               (*Enter* MICHAEL, *in driving gloves. He notices*
               HILDE.)

HILDE   What's that sound?

MICHAEL   (*confused*) Katie?

               (*There is an enormous explosion, very close
               by. When the dust settles,* HILDE *turns to*
               MICHAEL.)

HILDE   Not Katie, I'm afraid. (*Then back to the*
               OFFICER.) That . . .

               (*The* OFFICER *moves to get a better look. At
               length we realise: it is the sound of feet on the
               road – boots and shoes striking off the hard
               metalled surface. Hundreds and thousands of
               pairs of feet making their way steadily
               towards us. Walking without talking. The
               sound of pram wheels and carts.*)

OFFICER   (*in awe*) Jesus Christ . . .

(*A* MAN *appears – dirty, tired-looking. He is wearing an AFS armband.*)

MAN   (*quiet, distracted*) They're sending up bi-planes. Look – biplanes. Where's the bloody fighters?

OFFICER   (*reading the armband*) AFS. What you doing here?

MAN   (*puzzled*) What am I *doing* here?

(*The* MAN *collects himself.*)

MAN   I went in, the Climax, eight o'clock. A bomb hit a girder in the roof. About ten, the Chief and me, we was in the tool shop when that went up.

Then a blast. Biggest blast of the night. Goodbye test shop. Goodbye machine shop. Goodbye assembly shop. We get back to the hose. Main's gone. We switch to auxiliary. Nothing.

Then we see. The canal. Our auxiliary. Gone. Just . . . gone. *Everything*. The whole bloody city. Gone.

OFFICER   How many more are there like you?

(*The* MAN *moves the* OFFICER *to a better vantage point.*)

MAN   Try about 50,000? *What's happened to the bloody guns?*

(*Another massive explosion. Everyone flinches.* MICHAEL *approaches the* MAN.)

MICHAEL   (*quiet*) Do you know a place called Bramble Street?

MAN   Off Gosford Street?

MICHAEL   What's it like there?

MAN   Family there, have you?

MICHAEL   You could say that.

(*The* MAN *doesn't reply. He puts his hand on* MICHAEL'S *shoulder, thinks for a second, then starts walking.*)

HILDE   (*approaching* MICHAEL) My cab won't take me any further. Can you take me with you?

MICHAEL   (*still absorbing things*) In there?

HILDE   I'm game if you are . . .

(*A further huge blast rends the air. Lights fade.*)

Lights back up on the shelter at Bramble Street.

JOANIE   Mum –

MEG   What? (*Beat.*) What? (*Pause.*) You'll have to wait.

JOANIE   I can't.

MEG   You'll just have to –

JOANIE   Till when?

MEG   How do I know? Hitler didn't consult me personally.

(*A distant sound of bells chiming the half hour.*)

JACK   What's that?

MEG   It's the cathedral.

JOANIE   The *cathedral*?

MEG   It's funny isn't it? So clear, in spite of
               everything. (*She nudges* JACK.)

JACK   At least they didn't get that then.

               (*She nods her head.*)

JACK   What? (*Beat.*) She can do it in here can't she?

               (*She nods again.* JACK *slowly picks himself up,
               emerges from the shelter. Inside,* JOANIE *tries
               to use the pot.*)

JOANIE   Making me laugh . . .

MEG   Go on.

JOANIE   I can't – say water or something.

MEG   Niagara Falls.

JOANIE   I can't!

JACK   What's going on in there?

               (*There is a sudden, huge blast nearby.* JACK
               comes diving back into the shelter, as JOANIE
               re-arranges herself.)

JACK   It's like the Four Horsemen of the bloody
               Apocalypse.

MEG   Perhaps that's what it is. The End of the
               World.

JACK   Don't talk daft woman.

               (*A slight pause.*)

MEG   It's funny. I never told you what happened this
           morning. I was on my way to Sacred Heart –
           feeling guilty, because I hadn't been there all
           week – And I got half way there, and I
           remembered I needed something for Katie's
           birthday cake. So I thought – I thought I'll turn
           round and go back to Raglan Street – St Mary's
           – then I'll go *on* to Ball Hill after that. And it
           was only when I was there that I remembered.

JACK   Remembered what?

MEG   The last time I was there.

           Mrs Geraghty's eldest First Communion.
           Remember?

           We came home, and the Prime Minister was on
           the radio. 'No such undertaking.' . . . 'We are
           now at war with Germany.' So I ought to have
           known.

JACK   Ought to have known what?

MEG   God trying to tell me something.

JACK   Well if he's still there, ask him this – how much
           bloody longer is this going to go on.

JOANIE   (*cautioning*) Dad . . .

MEG   We upset him in so many different ways.

JACK   *We? We* upset him?

MEG   Fighting among ourselves. Is it any wonder
           he's angry?

           (*At this moment, a figure appears in the
           doorway, backlit by the almost daylight
           brightness from outside.*)

MEG   Ken . . .

(KEN *is covered in patches of red and some other, unidentifiable, substance.*)

KEN   (*quiet*) There's an ambulance . . . at the top of the street.

MEG   What's that on your coat?

KEN   On the way to Gulson Road. The driver and his mate caught the full force of one – by Charterhouse Street.

JOANIE   What is it?

KEN   There's a lady still alive in the back.

JOANIE   (*realising what it is on* KEN'S *coat, retching*) Jesus . . .

KEN   We need someone to take her to the hospital . . . (*Long pause.*) Jack, can you make it?

JACK   What about these?

KEN   These can look after themselves can't they?

JACK   (*beat*) I should stay here.

KEN   She'll die, Jack.

JACK   Take it.

KEN   What do you mean?

JACK   Take the car.

KEN   I'm not asking that . . . I'm asking *you* . . . you to take her. For Christ's sake . . . We've been sold down the river here. Hung out to fucking dry. There must be twenty thousand dead out there.

(JACK *weighs up the situaion, then, without a*
further word, gets up and goes out. KEN
follows, also wordlessly. Silence.)

JOANIE   (*quietly*) The problem with the guns is, they
          get hot. Then they stop firing. Everyone thinks
          they've run out of ammo.

MEG   (*beat*) You seem to know an awful lot about
          guns, all of a sudden.

          (*Silence.*)

          We should play another game.

JOANIE   I don't want to play another game. (*Pause.*)
          Ken shouldn't have a go at Dad like that.

MEG   Ken?

JOANIE   Dad drives me crackers sometimes. But he's not
          a coward. Going on about how it wasn't a very
          clever thing to do – get into an argument with
          his foreman . . .

MEG   We all do the best we can, don't we?

JOANIE   That's what people have been saying – isn't it?
          That Dad's a coward?

          (MEG *doesn't answer. The whine of a bomb.*
          MEG *gets up, slowly, and exits the shelter.*)

          Mum, what are you doing?

          (MEG *goes next door. Kneels, quietly, mutters*
          an inaudible prayer. Then gets up.)

MEG   I'm hungry. What about you? What about a
          bacon sandwich?

(*As she drifts in a daze towards the kitchen,
something catches her eye. Lights cross fade
with:*)

HILDE *and* MICHAEL. *The outskirts of the city. On the screen at
the back of the stage, a map shows the city slowly engulfed by
flame. The fires illuminate the characters' faces. It is as
bright, almost, as day.* HILDE *is unpacking some camera
equipment from a case.*

MICHAEL   I reckon that's as far as we get? What are you
                 doing?

HILDE   If we can't get any further, we can't get any
                 further.

MICHAEL   I meant . . . what are you *doing*?

HILDE   In the circumstances, this is the least I can do.
                 Here. Help me. It'll need a long exposure.

                 (*She sets up tripod, etc, and makes exposure.*)

                 We can try to get some kip over there,
                 afterwards.

                 (*Pause.*)

                 If this can happen here, in the middle of
                 England, people have got a right to ask why.
                 But before they can ask why, they need to see
                 what a thing like this looks like.

                 (*She offers* MICHAEL *her hip flask.*)

                 Don't you agree? (*Beat.*) You're rather cute,
                 aren't you, in your own way?

                 (MICHAEL *bats her hand away. Cross fade with
                 Bramble Street.*)

An air of exhaustion hangs over the shelter. MEG *plays with an old-fashioned fob watch.*

JOANIE   What have you got there?

MEG   I don't know why – Katie must have had it out . . .

JOANIE   The watch?

              (*Pause.*)

MEG   It's hard to imagine now, isn't it? At one time, in Craven Street, there were Adams' on both sides. Number 12, Number 25, Number 36, Number 42. Three generations of Adams' in one street. With the workshops on top.

JOANIE   I know, Mum.

              (*Beat.*)

              How come we've got it here?

MEG   (*reflective*) Made for a gentleman in London. Young lord, wanted the finest watch money could buy. In those days, that meant Coventry.

JOANIE   But he never took it?

MEG   Disappeared off the face of the Earth. To Australia, or somewhere.

JOANIE   Bastard.

MEG   Dad gave it to us for our wedding. (*A reverie.*) You should have seen us. Dad hired a car. A big old, green old Daimler. Like the one he'd had. We spent our wedding night at Kenilworth. Drove there . . . dead straight . . . along the Kenilworth Road. Felt like the richest

couple of swells in the world. (*Beat.*) The
money was long gone by then of course.

JOANIE   He could've gone into bicycles.

MEG   Bicycles?

JOANIE   Coventry can't blame the rest of the world for
            everything bad that happens to it can it?
            Change, or die, that's what Dad says isn't it?

            (*A sudden, ominous whine followed by a
            massive, massive explosion. Rubble descends
            onto the stage. Darkness.*)

JOANIE   (*eventually*) Mum. Mum? MUM?

MEG   (*faint*) I can hear you.

JOANIE   Are you alright?

MEG   I think so.

            (*Silence.*)

JOANIE   Blimey.

MEG   Are you hurt?

JOANIE   I don't know. I can't move.

            (JOANIE *begins to fumble for something. We
            hear the sound of scratching in the darkness.
            and then we see a flame – as she lights a
            match. The scene is one of absolute
            devastation. Bricks, and dust, glass and
            splintered wood.* JOANIE *lies pinned to the
            ground by a beam or a wooden doorpost. Her
            face is covered with blood.* MEG *lies still on
            the ground, some distance away.*)

JOANIE   Crikey!

MEG   Joanie . . .

                 (JOANIE *reaches for a hanky, pulls it out and
                 begins to dab, gently at her face. Panic.* KEN
                 enters.)

KEN   Jesus, Mary and Joseph.

JOANIE   Ken!

KEN   Are we alright? Is everyone alright?

JOANIE   I think so.

KEN   Meg?

                 (*She grunts.* KEN *moves to try to move the door
                 post pinning* JOANIE. *Strains, hard, but to no
                 avail.*)

                 (*Distracted.*) Hang on a minute, there'll be
                 someone –

JOANIE   What do you mean, someone?

KEN   Someone'll be here in a minute.

JOANIE   You're here, aren't you?

KEN   I can't shift it. (*Beat.*) There's a parachute mine
                 hanging between two chimneys in Terry Road.
                 There's about forty people trapped in a
                 basement. It could go at any moment.

JOANIE   So could we.

KEN   Hang on. (*This is agonising for* KEN.) Please
                 . . . just . . . hang on . . .

                 (*He goes. There are shouts, outside in the
                 street.*)

JOANIE   (*to herself*) Dear God. Dear sweet Lord . . .

(*Pause.*)

Mum, tell me something nice. You always used
to do that. If I couldn't sleep or if I was ill.
"Tell me something nice." And you'd sit, and
you'd tell me a story. The Three Billy Goats
Gruff. Or Snow White. Or Henley. You'd talk
about Henley. The garden at Aunty Vi's.

(*Turns her head.*) Your hair looks nice, by the
way. I forgot to tell you. Where did you get it
done? At Madge's?

(*Pause.*)

You remember when you used to do *my* hair?
Every night. Before bed. Then one day I had it
all cut off. Because you wouldn't let me have
piano lessons. Do you remember? Mum?

(*There is a noise.*)

Mum?

(*A new figure enters through the back door.
We see that the figure is wearing a child's
Mickey Mouse gas mask. The figure
approaches* JOANIE, *saying nothing. Stands
over her. Lights cross fade:*)

The Girdlers' Chapel of St Michael's Cathedral. PETER *enters,
carrying a piece of coloured cloth.*

PETER   If we're waiting, we might as well make
                 ourselves useful.

                 (*He hands* KATIE *an end of the material. She
                 reads.*)

KATIE   7th Battalion, The Royal Warwickshire
                 Regiment. What are we doing with this?

PETER   (*soothing*) Just folding it up.

KATIE   What's a Girdler?

PETER   Good question.

KATIE   A man who makes girdles?

PETER   I imagine.

KATIE   How come they get their own chapel?

PETER   (*beat*) It's funny isn't it – there haven't been girdlers in Coventry for 600 years. But here we still are.

KATIE   (*slaps the stone*) Built to last . . .

PETER   'Si monumentum requiris, circumspice.'

KATIE   What's that?

PETER   Two, three thousand years. 'Si monumentum requiris, circumspice.'

KATIE   But what does it mean?

PETER   If monument you require, look around you.

               (*In another space, the figure in the Mickey Mouse mask tears at* JOANIE'S *clothes.*)

JOANIE   (*terrified*) No. NO . . .

KATIE   That's the kind of thing Michael says.

               It's funny isn't it? Mum's a Catholic. She says the war's because we were horrid to the Germans after the last time. Dad's a Communist. He says it's the politicians and the businessmen. But . . . I don't know. What if it's *us*?

PETER   Us?

KATIE   All of us. Human beings. Everything beautiful
               we create. We destroy. It's inside us.

PETER   You don't believe that – do you?

KATIE   If I die tonight, there's so much I won't have
               done. So much I won't have seen.

               (*There is a enormous blast overhead. followed
               by a rending crack.*)

JOANIE   No. NO . . .

               (*There is a sudden rushing of flame.* PETER'S
               and KATIE'S *faces are suddenly illuminated. A
               penetrating scream fills the theatre.*)

PETER   (*speaking very quickly all of a sudden*) Our
               Father, Who art in Heaven, Hallowed be thy
               Name. Thy Kingdom Come/Thy Will be done,
               On earth as it is in Heaven.

               (*Another blast, then black.*)

*Lights slowly up on images of ashes and ruins, projected onto
the screen at the rear of the stage. Lights slowly up on stage.*
KATIE *lies in a hospital bed, her head bandaged.* MICHAEL
stands next to her. Unshaven. A long, long silence.

KATIE   When we were young, Dad made us a model
               town. Model houses, model fire station, model
               shops. Used to take up the whole of the back
               yard. All the buildings had roofs you could
               take off, and little people, inside, you could
               move around. You could imagine everything
               going on, the little stories, the people, who was
               married to who.

I used to play out in the street, walk up to the end there, where the shops are, and imagine what it was like. When that was one of the main ways into town. Coventry had walls, did you know that? And bridges. Two bridges. Between where we are, and where town is. I used to imagine the people, all the horses, the carriages.

MICHAEL   Katie . . .

KATIE   Gosford. Gooseford. Just like Oxford.

I used to imagine the excitement, as they passed the inns and the shops, on their way to market, wondering how much money they'd get, how many pennies, how many groats.

I used to imagine the city, when it was new. When the stone was all pink, not black. When the gold on top of the spires was sparkling bright. When the wood looked fresh-cut, and green. I used to imagine lots of things. But I never imagined this. (*Silence.*) How did you get here?

MICHAEL   A man in Bramble Street – Ken? – he was the one that told me – he said he came looking for you – asked at all the shelters, checked with control, talked to the police, finally found you here.

KATIE   I meant, how did you get here.

MICHAEL   To Coventry? I got as far as a place called Earlsdon. By car.

KATIE   But where did you spend the night?

MICHAEL   It's funny – (*He kicks himself – of course it isn't. Pause.*) In a girl guide hut. With a bunch of girl guides. And some newspaper men and women. Spent the night singing Ging Gang

Guly and Underneath the Spreading Chestnut
Tree.

KATIE   Have you seen my Dad?

MICHAEL   No. I haven't.

KATIE   I don't understand. *Ken said I should stay
             here, the best thing was to stay here. What did
             he mean by that?*

             (*Long pause.*)

MICHAEL   Have you had anything? Any food? A glass of
             water?

KATIE   You haven't kissed me yet.

MICHAEL   No, I . . .

KATIE   I feel such a fraud.

MICHAEL   Fraud?

KATIE   Lying here, useless, after what's happened.

MICHAEL   You were unconscious for a long time, the
             doctor said.

KATIE   But that was hours ago. Seems like days.
             Another life.

MICHAEL   Katie –

KATIE   What? (*Beat.*)

MICHAEL   What exactly did Ken tell you?

KATIE   We argued about you. Did you know that? My
             Dad said you wouldn't come.

MICHAEL   Katie –

KATIE   Mum said you would. (*Answering him.*) That
                   Mum was hurt. She'd been taken to Gulson
                   Road. They were doing the best they could . . .

MICHAEL   And what did you understand by that?

KATIE   (*pause*) That Ken was trying to be kind to me?

                   (*Pause.*)

MICHAEL   Is that all he told you?

KATIE   Yes. Why? Mum's dead, that's what you're
                   saying, isn't it? (*Puzzled.*) What else is there?

                   (MICHAEL *walks over to a window. Cannot –
                   yet – bring himself to tell her the other half of
                   the news. Lights fade.*)

Lights up on Bramble Street. The wreckage.

JACK *stands, still in the same clothes, and covered with grime.
He looks round the house. He picks up a few things, half-
heartedly. Where to even begin? He takes a chair, walking
through the debris, and out into the yard. There, he sits down,
reaches into a pocket, and pulls out a cigarette which he
lights, and smokes. There is a noise. The garden gate opens,
to admit a similarly shattered-looking* KEN, *who is carrying a
bottle of spirits.*

KEN   I generally make it a rule. Nothing before
                   eleven o'clock.

                   (JACK *doesn't reply.* KEN *enters the house,
                   searches and finds two beer glasses from the
                   previous night. He comes back out.*)

                   Looters, I reckon. Whole place is crawling with
                   them. Just lying in the middle of the road.

(*He empties the dregs before opening the bottle and filling the glasses with alcohol.*)

Joanie get off okay?

(JACK *nods, imperceptibly.*)

She'll be okay out there, with her auntie.

JACK   Where she should have been in the bloody first place.

(*He hands the glass to* JACK, *who holds his cigarette up for a light.*)

KEN   You wanna be careful. Cigarettes are bad for you.

JACK   At the hospital they asked me – is she allergic to anything? I told them yes – bombs.

KEN   She was a good woman, Jack.

JACK   I know that.

(KEN *places an arm on his shoulder.* JACK *takes a deep draw.*)

KEN   Some of the things I've seen. Honest to God. They'd break your heart. Nine members of one family in Bull Yard. The son just back on leave, he found them. A dog . . . a little dog . . . with a child's arm in its mouth. A bride and groom, in their wedding bed.

(*Beat.*)

Then some things just make you laugh . . . you can't help yourself . . . like your neighbour . . . Fag Ash Lil, the one with all the kids . . .

JACK   Netty?

KEN

I heard her just now, arguing with the AFS. 'What do you mean, you can't give me any water.' 'It's contaminated', he says. ' But my husband needs his tea. He can't do anything without his tea.'

JACK

Husband. That's a good one . . .

KEN

Then, this posh git turns up – vicar, teacher – (*Hoity toity.*) 'Is there anything I can do to help madam?' 'Yeah there is', she says. 'You can buy me a ticket to Aberystwyth.' 'But our duty is to stay here, isn't it, help put this city back on its feet.' 'Our duty to who, you arsehole? *Our duty to who?*'

(JACK *smiles, and then his smile fades. There is a noise – someone is coming in through the front door. It's* KATIE, *who stands for a moment to take in the scene in front of her. She walks through the house – as if in a trance – and towards the back door where she stands, quite still, for a moment.*)

KEN

That other thing you did. Don't think it wasn't appreciated. The lad whose wife it was – he's going to come and thank you, when he gets off his shift.

(*A beat, then* KEN *exits through the garden gate.* JACK *and* KATIE *stand and look at each other for a second –* JACK *looking searchingly at* KATIE *– what does she know? Then – when it is clear she knows everything – they come together, hold each other for a long time. They are interrupted by a second noise – the sound of the garden gate being opened again. We see* JOANIE *enter the yard and approach the back door.*)

JACK

(*astonished*) Joanie, what are you doing?

JOANIE

I got off at Tile Hill. Walked all the way back.

JACK   But why?

JOANIE   Because.

JACK   Love . . .

JOANIE   They've made quite a mess out there – haven't they?

JACK   Vi's expecting you. She's got a bed ready.

JOANIE   Dad, somebody raped me. I'm not an invalid.

            (*At the mention of the word, it's almost as if* JACK *has been struck. A pause, then* JOANIE *and* KATIE *hug.*)

            What about Michael. Did you hear anything about Michael?

KATIE   Michael came.

JOANIE   Oh Katie – I'm so thrilled. I'm so thrilled. What happened to him?

KATIE   I don't know . . .

JOANIE   So where is he now?

            (JOANIE *goes to the piano. She presses a key.*)

KATIE   He's missed the end of his leave. He had to try and get a message to someone . . .

            (*No sound emerges from the piano.*)

JOANIE   I'm so happy for you. I'm so happy.

            (*Fade.*)

MICHAEL *sits on a park bench. A* MAN *scrunches past, as if treading on broken glass.*

The drone of an aircraft is heard high up. The MAN *instinctively flinches. A van with a tannoy goes by, announcing something indistinct.*

A WOMAN *enters the space.* HILDE CHAMBERS (*the journalist*). *She stops in front of him.* (*each looks at the other: you again*). *She sits down.*

The two sit for a while in silence, before HILDE *offers* MICHAEL *a cigarette, which he takes, and she lights for him, before lighting her own.*

They smoke together in silence for a while.

HILDE   I managed to get five minutes with the Mayor, Jack Moseley, at the Council House. While I was there, who should fetch up to see him?

MICHAEL   Go on . . .

HILDE   Morrison and Beaverbrook themselves. Clean-shaven, pink-cheeked, in their office best.

MICHAEL   *Here*, in Coventry?

HILDE   (*with an ironic flourish*) 'The roots of the Air Force are planted in Coventry', says one. 'If Coventry's output is destroyed the tree will languish. But if the city rises from the ashes, then the tree will burgeon, putting forth fresh leaves and branches. I'm looking for an all-out effort from Coventry.'

                    This, after walking through *these* streets! People walking, with their possessions piled up in wheelbarrows. People queuing for food, and shelter. People fighting over loaves.

                    'I want these factories running as soon as is humanly possible', says Beaverbrook.

'Or what?' says the Mayor.

'Or we shall have to find men who are capable
of doing it for you.'

(MICHAEL'S *face clenches with fury as the
meaning of this last sinks in. Lights fade.*)

While KATIE *and* JOANIE *salvage what they can from the house
– the odd piece of furniture, small ornaments, bits of food –*
JACK *tinkers with the shattered piano under the stairs.
Suddenly, he stands up, nursing his thumb.*

JACK   Shit. Bugger . . .

(*He walks round the room in a state of
agitated frustration. In this hiatus,* KATIE
*suddenly notices something on the ground,
which she bends to pick it up. It's the watch.
Still sucking his thumb,* JACK *goes to the
radio. Presses a button – more in hope than in
expectation. But is astonished when the it lets
out a huge farting noise, and slowly comes
into life.*)

VOICE   (*Lord Haw Haw-ish, a quisling tone*) 'Well,
workers, it's hard luck on Coventry and, of
course, it's hard luck on the workers . . . most
people thought it wouldn't be too easy to
smash up one of the biggest production bases
in the country but it was and the main question
now is 'How was it allowed to happen?" * The
morale in the city is broken. Quite, quite
broken . . .

JACK   (*rising anger*) Bloody bastards. Bloody
traitorous bastards.

* NB this is an actual broadcast by 'Workers' Challenge', a
'black' propaganda station aimed at the British Working Class.

(JACK *changes station. this time finding the honeyed tones of an obviously BBC announcer. The girls are surprised by this sudden and ferocious outburst.*)

RADIO   'Splintered and battered as they were, shops and offices opened at the usual time. Al fresco shopping and roadside trading continued during the morning, while fire brigades, demolition units and rescue squads worked heroically, quelling fires and extricating people trapped beneath the debris . . .'

(*There is a noise, as* KEN *enters through the garden gate. Everyone just stands and stares. For some reason,* KEN *can't look them in the eye.* JACK *turns the radio down.*)

KATIE   Well?

KEN   (*beat*) You might have heard this already?

KATIE   Heard what?

KEN   They're saying . . . (*He pauses.*) . . . they're saying no private burials . . . except for people who lived outside the city . . .

JACK   No private burials?

         What does that mean?

         (*Long pause.*)

JOANIE   We'll see Mum again, shan't we, before the funeral?

         (*Pause.*)

KEN   It's been decided.

JACK   By who? By who?

JOANIE   We can go to the place where she's laid out, can't we?

KEN   (*overcome*) There was an explosion . . . the gasworks next to the morgue . . . took the roof off. All the number tags have gone in the rain . . . they're not letting anyone in . . .

(*They begin to absorb the desperate finality of this.*)

Oh, and here's the nice thing . . . anyone who has any objection . . . or anyone who doesn't want to work . . . they're saying they'll *send the troops in* . . .

(*A sense of palpable rage descends on the room. A knock at the front door. No one moves. Another knock. At length,* KATIE *goes to open it.*)

KATIE   Michael –

MICHAEL   (*entering*) I knocked earlier. But there was no reply . . . (*Silence. He takes in the situation.*) Sorry. I didn't mean – (*To interrupt.*)

KATIE   It's okay . . .

(*Silence.*)

Ken just came to tell us something.

(*Everyone stands and stares at* MICHAEL.)

JACK   You'll be needing to get back to your work, won't you lad?

MICHAEL   What?

JACK   You'll be needing to get back to your work.

MICHAEL   Actually, I'm not sure what I'll need to be
                  doing . . .

                  (*Everyone continues to stare at* MICHAEL.
                  *Then, people begin to drift away, finding
                  different ways to process their grief.* KATIE *and*
                  MICHAEL *are left, momentarily, alone. Silence.*)

MICHAEL   There's a policeman outside. He's here to
                  speak to Joanie. I said it was a good idea to
                  wait. Did I do the right thing?

KATIE   (*beat*) Yes, Michael. You did the right thing.

                  (KATIE *is staring at him, intently.*)

                  What's the matter? What's the matter?

                  (MICHAEL *doesn't reply. As the lights dim, an
                  eery, not quite earthly sound echoes around
                  the auditorium: the children, singing 'The Big
                  Ship Sails in the Alley Alley-oh'.*)

MICHAEL *catches up with* MORRISON *in the street. A man with
pink scrubbed cheeks and a clean suit.*

MICHAEL   Mr Morrison?

MORRISON   (*turning*) Yes?

MICHAEL   Mr Morrison?

MORRISON   What is it?

MICHAEL   (*beat*) I hope your conscience is as clean as
                  your suit.

MORRISON   I beg your pardon?

MICHAEL   Sic transit Gloria mundi.

MORRISON   What's that you say?

MICHAEL   Thus passes the glory of the world.

MORRISON   I know what it means lad. *But why do you say it?*

MICHAEL   Because you knew, didn't you? You bloody well knew. And you did nothing.

MORRISON   If you'll excuse me, we've work to do here. Hard work.

            (MICHAEL *sinks to his knees.*)

            What's the matter lad? Are you hurt? Have you lost somebody?

            (MICHAEL *breaks down and sobs. The sound of a ambulance siren passes somewhere offstage.*)

MICHAEL   (*to himself*) My conscience hath a thousand several tongues/ And every tongue brings in a several tale/And every tale condemns me for a villain . . . Where wilt thou find a cavern dark enough/To mask thy monster's visage?

            (MICHAEL *is lost. Lights fade.*)

Behind MICHAEL, *the world of the play now slowly begins to disappear. The elements of the set – the house at Bramble Street and the few details of the hut – are borne away – until – if possible – the stage is completely bare.*

As MICHAEL *stares into space, we see, projected on the screen at the back, the front cover of an american newspaper – the New York Herald Tribune, which carries a picture of the devastated shell of St Michael's Cathedral, and the headline:*

The Unfathomable Brutality.

Then alongside:

'No means of defence which the United States can place in British hands should be witheld'.

Slowly, the stage begins to fill with mourners (other cast and members of the company), until finally, they are joined by JACK, KATIE, JOANIE *and* KEN.

MICHAEL *leaves the stage.* KATIE *looks in vain for him.*

A voice is heard.

VOICE   Almighty God, with whom do live the spirits of them that depart hence in the Lord, and with whom the souls of the faithful, after they are delivered from the burden of the flesh, are in joy and felicity. We remember before thee now all those whose names are before us, beseeching thee, that it may please thee, of thy gracious goodness, shortly to accomplish the number of thine elect.

       Let us go out and try to live unbroken and unembittered, asking the help of God's Holy Spirit to strengthen us that these dead may be prouder of us when we meet again.

       We commend those whom we love to the mercy and care of God, our Heavenly Father. Let us depart in peace.

       (KEN *leans to* JACK. KATIE *continues to search for* MICHAEL *with her eyes.*)

KEN   (*SV*) So what now?

JACK   What now? The only thing I know how. Build magnetos for aircraft engines.

KEN   You can knock a man down. And you can kick him when he's down. But he can still get up again.

JACK   Ay, he can that.

                (KATIE *looks again for* MICHAEL, *but he is not there. She is devastated. Lights slowly fade.*)

KATIE *steps forward, tieing her hair up, as at the beginning of the play*

JOHN MARTIN *enters. They stand in silence for a moment. We are back in 1976.*

KATIE   (*measured*) You see, we're quite used to the idea in Coventry that we're off, or under the radar . . . that decisions get taken . . . in Berlin, in New York, in Whitehall . . . a decision gets taken and we get to live with that decision . . . But *this?*

                (MARTIN *absorbs this.*)

MARTIN   (*deliberate*) *Was* there a place where people like your friend were employed? Yes. *Might* there have been some advance knowledge? (*Pause.*) It's possible. Did what happened to your friend happen because of this, or for a different reason entirely? (*Beat.*) That, I am afraid, I cannot tell you.

KATIE   But one thing keeps coming back to me.

MARTIN   Yes?

KATIE   The one thing everyone *can* agree on – all the different people who've been talking, and writing – the one thing everyone *can* agree is the beams. That, by three o'clock on the day, the beams were intersecting over the city. And yet *you* say that he told *you* the beams were indicating London.

MARTIN   That is my recollection, yes.

KATIE   Your recollection . . .

MARTIN   What are you . . . a journalist . . . *what*?

KATIE   Not a journalist. A teacher. A simple teacher of
               children . . .

MARTIN   But what do you hope to *gain* by this?

               (*Pause.*)

KATIE   When I was young, I knew nothing. Then . . . I
               saw what I wanted to see. Now . . . what it's
               always been about, for me, is why?

*There is a gradual change in the lighting state. We are now
back in 1941, in the grounds of a nursing home, somewhere in
the eastern Home Counties. The sound of birdsong.* MARTIN
steps to one side.

Enter MICHAEL, *now dressed in cords, pajamas and a dressing
gown. He stands with his hands in his pockets, staring into
space.*

KATIE *releases her hair once more and steps forward. We see
that she is carrying a brown paper bag with a stalk of grapes
protruding.*

KATIE   Listen.

               (*Beat.*)

               It's so quiet . . .

               (*Beat.*)

               Not like Coventry. Honestly Michael, you
               wouldn't believe it. Three months since the
               bombs, and you'd hardly recognise the place . . .
               cranes, earth-movers, diggers . . .

(*Beat.*)

I brought you these. Not very original, I know.
But you don't smoke, and you're not supposed
to drink. So . . . (*Grapes it is.*)

(MICHAEL *does not reply.*)

Joanie sends her love. (*Beat.*) We're to have a
new house. Did I say that in the letter?
Michael, you should see it. Three bedrooms! A
bath! And a *garden!* An actual garden with
flowers in it. Lobelias. Chrysanthemums.
Geraniums . . .

(*Beat.*)

MICHAEL   (*almost to himself*) 'A gallant curtle axe upon
her thigh, a boar spear in her hand . . .'

(*Pause.*)

KATIE   You must be wondering how I found you.

(*Beat.*)

It wasn't hard. I remembered where it was you
said your family were. The jewellers, in the
High Street, in Smethwick. I looked in the
telephone directory, for Greens, in Birmingham.
Worked my way through one by one, until I
found you. And then, I came. I came to find
you. Just like you came to find me.

(*Pause.*)

I was so cross with you Michael. You didn't
come to the Burial . . . you didn't ring me . . .
and my *letters* . . . you didn't answer any of my
letters . . .

(MICHAEL *doesn't reply.*)

But I understand now. I understand. About
your illness. That your work . . . you'd been
working so hard . . . everything just got on top
of you . . .

(*Long pause.*)

(*deep breath*) Michael . . . Joanie said that that
night, the night of the bombs, Mum told her
there was a phone call. Somebody rang the
phone, the phone rang out, but when she
picked it up, there was nobody there . . .
Michael . . . was that you?

(*Pause.*)

Was it?

(*Long pause.*)

Michael I was so excited. I'd had a letter. From
St Hilda's College, in Oxford. Saying they
wanted to meet me. Me, they wanted to meet
me . . .

(*Pause.*)

Michael, you do understand, don't you? We
stayed, in Coventry, for you.

(*Still* MICHAEL *says nothing.*)

Speak to me Michael. *Say something to me.*
What's Shakespeare got to say about this?
What's Schiller, or Schlegel, or Tieck?

(*There is a noise.* SHEILA *enters, clutching a
bunch of grapes.*)

SHEILA   Well, I wouldn't say it was worth le detour, but
still, an improvement on your last place of
incarceration. (*Seeing* KATIE.) Oh –

(*Beat.*)

I'm sorry –

I'm Sheila. You're –

KATIE   Katie.

(*Pause.*)

SHEILA   Ah, Katie. (*Realising.*) Katie . . .

(*Long pause, as* KATIE *looks from one to the other.*)

KATIE   Well . . . (*Struggling to master her emotions.*) if you ever want to come and see us Michael . . . you know where we are. (*Beat.*) You'll find things aren't as bad as you think. All the little shops sprung up . . . (*She's crying now.*) . . . the factories back working . . . and the plans, Michael! You should see the plans! We're to have houses, schools . . . a road round the city in the sky! They say Coventry'll be a beacon to the world.

(*Finally, she can bear it no longer.*)

I just hope you understand what you did.

(*She runs out. Silence.* SHEILA *comes and stands by* MICHAEL.)

SHEILA   Courage, mon brave. Courage.

MICHAEL   (*finally*) 'And in this seat of peace Tumultuous Wars/Shall Kin with Kin and Kind with Kind Confound/Disorder, Horror, Fear and Mutiny shall here Inhabit/And this Land be called the Field of Golgotha . . .'

(MICHAEL *starts to shake.*)

SHEILA   Michael?

(*But* MICHAEL *is unreachable. The lights slowly fade.*)

End of play.